Tic-Tac-Toe Math

DAVE CLARK

DALE SEYMOUR PUBLICATIONS

Illustrations: Jeffrey Clark

Order number DS21107
ISBN 0-86651-547-X

10 11 12 13 14 MA 05 04 03 02 01

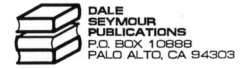

DALE
SEYMOUR
PUBLICATIONS
P.O. BOX 10888
PALO ALTO, CA 94303

Contents

Introduction

Designed for grades 5-8, each *Tic-Tac-Toe Math* game sheet contains nine problems in a tic-tac-toe format. Most of the problems focus on a common concept such as decimal computation, metric or standard measurements, percent operations, math vocabulary, probability, and area and perimeter. The problem in the center of the game is more complex and involves problem-solving strategies such as guess and check, look for a pattern, and work backward.

How to Use

Tic-Tac-Toe Math game masters may be used as 10-minute starter activities at the beginning of math class or as "fillers." They also may be used as short review activities, extra credit challenges, or even as assignments for specific topics. (The Skills Planner on page vi will help you select game sheets for specific skills.) The game sheets may be used by individual students, pairs of students, or small groups.

How to Score

Students receive 1 point for each correct solution plus 1 bonus point for each "tic-tac-toe" (3 correct solutions in a row, column, or diagonal). Students may earn a maximum of 17 points if all problems within a game are solved correctly. See page 89 for the Answer Key.

Tic-Tac-Toe Math allows teachers to:

- review and reinforce math concepts throughout the year.
- teach problem solving every day.
- provide extra-credit activities that bring more variety to each class session.
- teach and reinforce math vocabulary.
- present concepts in an integrated way.
- provide practice in a motivating, enjoyable format.
- keep concepts in all areas fresh in the minds of students.

Skills Planner

Skill	Game Number	Skill	Game Number
Algebra	56, 57, 58, 59, 60, 61, 62	Multiples	18
		Number Theory	16, 17, 18, 19, 20, 21, 22
Angles	45, 47		
Area	41, 42	Order of Operations	5
Circles	43		
Circumference	42	Percent	35, 36, 37, 38, 39
Comparisons	9	Perimeter	41
Decimals	26, 27, 30, 31, 32	Polygons	48
Division	31	Prime Numbers	18
Equations	60	Probability	54, 55
Estimation	14, 15	Problem Solving	49, 50, 51
Exponents	16, 17	Proportion	33
Factors	18	Rate	34
Fractions	23, 24, 25, 26, 27, 28, 29, 30, 36	Ratio	33
		Sequences	18, 22
Functions	61, 62	Simple Interest	11
Geometry	47, 48	Statistics	52, 53
Graphing	56	Surface Area	43
Integers	57, 58, 59	Time	12, 13
Jobs	10	Variables	60
Lines	47	Vocabulary	6
Measurement	39, 40, 41, 42, 43, 44, 45, 46	Volume	43
		Whole Numbers	1, 2, 3, 4, 5, 6
Money	7, 8, 9, 10, 11		

Whole Numbers

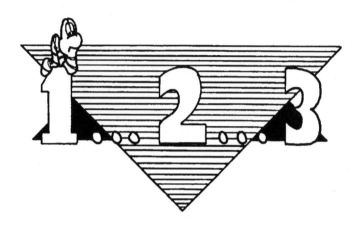

Game 1

$\boxed{}$ $\times\, 8$ ———— 7992	If you write all whole numbers from 1 to 100, how many times will you write the digit 5?	821 $-\, \boxed{}$ ———— 433
$2 + 5 \times 7 - 7 =$	If 4 airplanes land at an airport every 5 minutes, how many airplanes land at the airport in 1 day?	$17 + \boxed{} = 51$
$(\boxed{} + 5) \times 4 = 300$	26,456 $-\, 9,527$ ————	$\boxed{}\,\overline{)900}$ 15

© Dale Seymour Publications

Game 2

$60 \div (5 + 7) + 50 =$	What number do you multiply by 18 to get a product of 432?	$15 \div 3 \times 8 - 2 =$
Start with _____ . Subtract 7. Add 9. The result is 22.	What is the sum of all whole numbers 1 to 40?	$18\overline{)36,072}$
$75 + 39 \times 2 - 1 =$	$\begin{array}{r} 9887 \\ 5694 \\ + 8917 \\ \hline \end{array}$	$18 - 15 + 6 \div 3 =$

© Dale Seymour Publications

Game 3

256 + ▯ ――― 943	5108 − ▯ ――― 799	I bowled 5 games. My scores were 150, 145, 160, 138, and 172. What was my average?

1 → 1
2 → 4
3 → 9
4 → ▯
	If A = 1
	   B = 3
	   C = 6
	   D = 10
	
	and if the pattern continues, what is the letter H worth?
		1 → 1
		2 → 8
		3 → 27
		4 → 64
		
		What rule explains this?

$42 \div N = 6$ N = ▯	What number is 3000 less than 82,049?	In this number, circle the millions place. 3,059,214,756

Game 4

$\square - 23 = 15$	If you are now 12 years old, how old will you be in 11 years?	What is a consecutive number?
I am thinking of a number. If you multiply it by 9 and then subtract 4, the answer is 41. What is my number?	Use each number only once. Add, subtract, multiply, or divide to get an answer of 3. Use all numbers. Show how. 8 6 5 9 1	What three consecutive numbers give a sum of 81 when added?
$\begin{array}{r}\square \\ \times\ 8 \\ \hline 96 \end{array}$	What number comes next? 98, 97, 95, 92, 88	A team played 27 games. It won 5 more games than it lost. How many games did the team win?

Game 5

$5 + 3 \cdot 2 + 12 =$	$8 \div 2 + 4 \div 2 =$	$36 \div (9 - 3) + 2^2 =$
$(3 + 2) \cdot (5 + 4) =$	Add parentheses to make this true. $12 + 96 \div 6 - 4 = 24$	$2^2 + 4 - 2^3 \div 4 =$
$4 + 2^3 - 12 \div 3 =$	$(3 + 1)^2 - 8 \cdot 2 =$	$2^2 \cdot (3^3 + 4^2) =$

© Dale Seymour Publications

Game 6

I am thinking of two numbers Their sum is 15. Their difference is 3. What are the numbers?	What is a sum?	The sum of two numbers is 16. The product of the two numbers is 39. What are the numbers?
What is a product?	The product of two whole numbers is 72. When the first number is added to 3 times the second, the answer is 42. What are the two numbers?	What is a difference?
The difference of two numbers is 6. The quotient of the two numbers is 3 if you divide the smaller into the larger. What are the two numbers?	What is a quotient?	What two numbers give a product of 12 and a quotient of 3?

© Dale Seymour Publications

Money

Game 7

Give change from a $5.00 bill: ball-point pen, $0.87 toothpaste, $1.69	Dad pays me $5 for A grades and $4 for B grades. I pay him $2 for a D and $5 for an F. My grades were A A D F B. What did Dad pay me?	Give change from a $20.00 bill: calculator, $7.98 disc, $4.99
I work 23 hours at $8.50 per hour. How much do I earn?	Sandwiches: $1.25 Apples: $0.60 Milk: $0.65 I bought some of each. I got $5.05 back from a $10.00 bill. What did I buy?	Tennis balls sell for $2.67 per can. There are 3 balls in each can. How much do 2 balls cost?
I start with $123.00 in my checking account. I write checks for $17.50, $39.85, and $52.28. Then I deposit $65.00. How much is in my checking account now?	I want to buy 5 cups of yogurt at 65¢ each. How much will I get back from a $10 bill?	I want to buy a car for $1150.00. I earn $5.25 per hour. How many hours must I work to buy the car if all my earnings go for this purchase?

Game 8

I earn $12.00 in 5 hours. At this rate, how many hours will it take to earn $19.20?	How many nickels equal $18.45?	I earn $20.00 in 4 hours. At this rate, how much will I earn in 28 hours?
[box] + $3.59 [box] − $0.47 $5.59 What is the number in the top box?	You buy 144 inches of ribbon at 15¢ per yard and $3\frac{1}{2}$ pounds of tomatoes at 48¢ per pound. What is your change from a $20 bill?	How many quarters equal $20.75?
How many dimes equal $12.60?	Gasoline costs $1.29 per gallon. How much will it cost to fill a 15-gallon tank?	I sell hot dogs at a football game. I can make a hot dog for $0.65 and sell it for $1.00. If I sell 50 hot dogs, what is my profit?

Game 9

Which is less expensive? $0.80 for 2 lbs or $1.80 for 3 lbs	Which is more expensive? 4 at $0.24 each or 2 at $0.47 each	Which is the better buy? Store A $250 at 20% off or Store B $280 at 25% off
Which is the better buy? Store A $180 at $\frac{1}{3}$ off or Store B $110 at 10% off	I earn $12.00 in 5 hours. At this rate, how many hours will it take to earn $19.20?	If tuna sells at 3 cans for $2.31, what is the price of 1 can?
A six-pack of juice sells for $2.28. What does 1 can cost?	Which is the higher rate of pay? **a.** $12.00 for 5 hours **b.** $43.00 for 20 hours **c.** $24.50 for 10 hours	A store is giving a refund of 5¢ for every aluminum can returned. I bring in 56 cans. How much do I get for the cans?

Game 10

What is gross pay?	What is net pay?	I work 30 hours at $4.75 per hour. What is my gross pay?
I work $8\frac{1}{2}$ hours on Monday, $6\frac{3}{4}$ hours on Tuesday, and 7 hours on Wednesday. If I earn $7.60 per hour, what is my gross pay?	I get time and a half if I work overtime. This means I earn $1\frac{1}{2}$ times my hourly wage for hours after 40. How much is earned for 45 hours at $4.50 per hour?	What is the gross pay for working 8.2 hours at $5.50 per hour?
My net pay was $115.65 after deductions were taken. Deductions were $35.25. What was my gross pay?	How many hours did I work if I earned $137.80 at $5.30 per hour?	My net pay this week is $80. My gross pay is $100. What percent of my gross pay represents what was deducted?

Game 11

What is principal (in relation to borrowing money)?	What is interest?	What is rate (in relation to borrowing money)?
Write the formula for finding simple interest. _____ x _____ x _____	I borrow $1560 at a rate of 14% for 3 years (simple interest). How much will I pay each month if the loan is divided into equal monthly payments?	Find simple interest. principal = $900 rate = 11% time = 2 years
Find simple interest. principal = $1200 rate = 8% time = $1\frac{1}{2}$ years	I borrowed $650 at 10% interest. I paid it back in 6 months. How much did it cost me to borrow this money?	principal = $2200 rate = 6% time = 2 years What will be the total amount I must pay on this loan?

Time

Game 12

If October 2 is on a Tuesday, on what day will October 15 be?	2 hours 10 minutes – 1 hour 40 minutes _____ _____ hours _____ minutes	It is 8:30 PM. What time will it be 10 hours from now?
How many seconds are in 1 day?	An airplane leaves Portland, Oregon, at 7:00 AM and flies to Wichita, Kansas. What time do the airport clocks show at Wichita if the trip took $3\frac{1}{2}$ hours?	How many minutes are in 1 day?
How many weeks are in 1 year?	How many days are in 1 leap year?	Name the months that have exactly 30 days.

© Dale Seymour Publications

Game 13

(Answer in the lowest terms.) 2 hours 45 minutes + 3 hours 35 minutes _____ hours _____ minutes	(Use lowest terms.) 5 years 6 months + 8 years 9 months _____ years _____ months	It is 9:00 AM in Seattle, Washington. What time is it in New York City?
It is 7:00 PM in Houston, Texas. What time is it in Los Angeles, California?	The telephone company charges $1.35 for the first 3 minutes of a phone call and $0.35 for each additional minute. I talk on the phone from 4:17 PM until 4:31 PM. What will the phone call cost?	My clock shows that it is 8:40 AM. What time will it be in $6\frac{1}{2}$ hours?
How many minutes are in 3.5 hours?	450 minutes equals how many hours?	It is now 6:30 AM. What time was it $8\frac{1}{2}$ hours ago?

Estimation

Game 14

Round to the nearest cent. $1.6845	Round to the nearest tenth. 5.9478	Round to the nearest unit (one). 8.0546
Round to the nearest thousandth. 2.0547	Which is the best rate of pay? $19.80 for $5\frac{1}{2}$ hours or $38 for 10 hours or $42 for 12 hours	Round to the nearest ten. 24.75
Round to the nearest dollar. $125.39	Estimate: $0.19 x 4 is about _____ .	Round to the nearest hundred. 1728.55

Game 15

At a supermarket, a pound of ground beef would cost **a.** less than $1.00. **b.** about $1.50. **c.** about $1.75. **d.** $2.00 or more.	A gallon of milk would cost **a.** less than $1.00. **b.** about $1.25. **c.** about $1.50. **d.** between $1.75 to $2.00. **e.** more than $2.00.	A loaf of whole-wheat bread would cost **a.** about $0.75. **b.** about $1.00. **c.** about $1.25. **d.** about $1.50. **e.** more than $1.50.
A package of three #2 pencils would cost **a.** about 20¢. **b.** about 30¢. **c.** about 40¢. **d.** about 50¢. **e.** more than 50¢.	About how much do you think your teacher's shoes cost? **a.** less than $25 **b.** $26 to $35 **c.** $36 to $45 **d.** $46 to $55 **e.** more than $55	The average cost for a dozen large eggs is **a.** about $0.50. **b.** $0.60 to $0.75. **c.** $0.80 to $1.00. **d.** more than $1.00.
About how much would a 6-pack of juice cost? **a.** less than $1.00 **b.** $1.00 to $1.49 **c.** $1.50 to $1.99 **d.** $2.00 or more	About how much does a pound of carrots cost? **a.** $0.30 to $0.79 **b.** $0.80 to $1.09 **c.** $1.10 to $1.39 **d.** $1.40 to $1.79 **e.** $1.80 or more	About how much does a bar of soap cost? **a.** about $0.25 **b.** $0.26 to $0.49 **c.** $0.50 to $0.89 **d.** $0.90 to $1.10 **e.** $1.11 or more

Number Theory

Game 16

What is a square number?	What is the sum of the first eight square numbers?	What is an exponent?
Write the exponent. $64 = 8^{\square}$	How many squares are shown here? 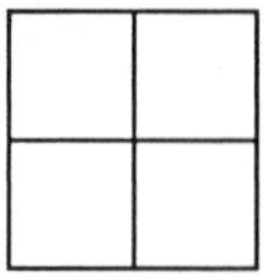	Write the exponent. $27 = 3^{\square}$
$81 = \square^2$	$5^3 =$	$300 = 3 \times \square^2$ (x means "multiply" in this problem.)

Tic-Tac-Toe Math

Game 17

$8 = \boxed{}^3$	$3^3 =$	$4^3 =$
$100 = \boxed{}^2$	I earn 1¢ on Jan. 1. I earn 2¢ on Jan. 2. I earn 4¢ on Jan. 3. I earn 8¢ on Jan. 4. If this pattern continues, how much will I earn on Jan. 15?	$2^3 =$
$27 = \boxed{}^3$	$10^2 =$	$64 = \boxed{}^3$

Tic-Tac-Toe Math

Game 18

List all the factors of 72.	List the first six multiples of 8.	List all the factors of 40.
List the first six multiples of 6.	I am thinking of a number between 20 and 50. It is an even number. It has exactly 9 factors. What is my number?	What is the least common multiple of 6 and 8?
What is the greatest common factor of 40 and 72?	Write the prime numbers less than 20.	What is a prime number?

Game 19

Write 12.34 x 10^4 in standard form.	Write 6256 in expanded form.	Write 5000 in scientific notation.
Write all factors of 24.	Write all prime numbers between 20 and 40.	In which example is 6 the product? **a.** 5 + 1 = 6 **b.** 9 − 3 = 6 **c.** 6 x 3 = 18 **d.** 2 x 3 = 6 **e.** 18 ÷ 3 = 6
Which number is deficient? **a.** 6 **b.** 12 **c.** 10	Which number is perfect? **a.** 6 **b.** 9 **c.** 16	Which number is composite? **a.** 2 **b.** 3 **c.** 4 **d.** 5

Game 20

Which number is square? **a.** 3 **b.** 10 **c.** 16 **d.** 21	Write the prime factorization of 100. (Use exponents.)	Which number is not a multiple of 4? **a.** 12 **b.** 20 **c.** 6 **d.** 28
Which number is abundant? **a.** 6 **b.** 10 **c.** 12	List the proper factors of 8.	6 is a factor of what number? **a.** 2 **b.** 10 **c.** 12 **d.** 8
$10^3 =$ **a.** 30 **b.** 100 **c.** 1000	Is 1 a prime number?	Write 4225 in scientific notation.

Game 21

I am composite. I have 2 digits. I have 8 factors. I am 1 less than a square number. What number am I?	I am prime. If you multiply my 2 digits, the product is a square number. What number am I? (Find three solutions.)	List the first six square numbers.
Write the prime factorization of 36. Use exponents.	What two numbers have a GCF of 5 and a LCM of 50?	List the first four triangular numbers.
What is the first number greater than 1 that is both a square number and a triangular number?	When you multiply my digits, the product is 20. When you add my digits, the sum is a square number. What number am I?	Write the prime factorization of 50. Use exponents.

Game 22

Write the next three numbers in the sequence. 1, 4, 7, 10,	Write the next three numbers. 3, 6, 12, 24,	Write the next three numbers. 1, 3, 6, 10,
Write the next three numbers. $\frac{1}{2}$, $\frac{1}{4}$, $\frac{1}{8}$,	Write the next three numbers. 1, 4, 9, 16,	Write the next three numbers. 0.3, 0.6, 0.9,
What three letters come next? A, Z, B, Y,	What three figures come next? ○ □ △ ○	Write the next three numbers. 5, 3, 1,

Tic-Tac-Toe Math

Fractions
and Decimals

and

Ratio,
Proportion,
and Percent

Game 23

What is the top part of a fraction called?	Which fraction is larger: five-eighths or three-fourths?	What is a denominator?
Write this fraction in lowest terms. $\frac{9}{12} =$	Which of these fractions is equivalent to $\frac{3}{4}$? $\frac{6}{8}, \frac{12}{16}, \frac{4}{6}, \frac{9}{12}, \frac{75}{100}, \frac{16}{20}$	Which of these fractions is an improper fraction? $\frac{5}{3}$ or $\frac{3}{5}$
Write a decimal for $\frac{3}{4}$.	Change $\frac{5}{3}$ to a mixed number.	Which part of a fraction tells how many parts it takes to make a whole? (numerator or denominator?)

Name_____

Game 24

What is $\frac{1}{12}$ of a dozen?	$\frac{1}{3} + \frac{1}{4} =$	$\frac{1}{6}$ of a dozen =
$\frac{1}{3} + \frac{1}{6} + \frac{1}{12} =$	I am thinking of a number. $\frac{1}{12}$ of it equals 6. $\frac{1}{3}$ of it equals_____.	$\frac{1}{6} + \frac{1}{12} =$ Write the answer in lowest terms.
What is $\frac{1}{4}$ of a dozen?	$\frac{1}{4} + \frac{1}{6} + \frac{1}{3} =$ Write the answer in lowest terms.	$\frac{1}{3}$ of a dozen =

© Dale Seymour Publications

Tic-Tac-Toe Math

33

Game 25

$\frac{5}{8} \times \frac{2}{3} =$ Write the answer in lowest terms.	Circle the greatest number. $\frac{5}{8}$ $\frac{2}{3}$ $\frac{3}{4}$	 What fraction does the letter A represent?
$1\frac{7}{8} =$ Write an improper fraction.	I am less than $\frac{3}{4}$ but more than $\frac{1}{2}$. My numerator and denominator are both square numbers. What fraction am I?	$5\overline{)27}$ Write the quotient as a mixed number.
$\begin{array}{r} 5\frac{5}{6} \\ -2\frac{3}{4} \\ \hline \end{array}$	What is $\frac{2}{3}$ of 60?	$\frac{25}{3} =$ Write the answer as a mixed number.

© Dale Seymour Publications

Tic-Tac-Toe Math

Name _____

Game 26

What is the sum of 0.5 and $\frac{3}{4}$?	Write 0.5 as a fraction in lowest terms.	What is the product of 0.5 and $\frac{3}{4}$?
Write $\frac{3}{4}$ as a decimal.	John has $\frac{3}{4}$ as many baseball cards as Mario. Mario has 60 cards. How many cards does John have?	$\frac{3}{4} \div 0.5 =$
What is $\frac{3}{4}$ of a dollar?	What is $\frac{3}{4}$ of a dozen?	I have a sack of rocks that weighs 8 pounds. Each rock weighs 0.5 pounds. How many rocks are in the sack?

© Dale Seymour Publications

Game 27

Write three-tenths as a fraction. Write three-tenths as a decimal.	Write fifteen hundredths as a fraction. Write fifteen hundredths as a decimal.	The decimal for $\frac{6}{1000}$ is written as _____ .
Write three and three ten-thousandths as a decimal.	Write a decimal that is exactly halfway between 0.5 and 0.6.	Write a fraction in lowest terms for 0.50.
Write 0.008 as a fraction. (not lowest terms)	Write $5\frac{8}{10,000}$ as a decimal.	Write 7.05 as a mixed number in lowest terms.

Game 28

Shade in $\frac{2}{3}$ of the circles. ⭘⭘⭘⭘⭘⭘ ⭘⭘⭘⭘⭘⭘	Shade in $\frac{3}{4}$ of the circles. ⭘⭘⭘⭘⭘⭘ ⭘⭘⭘⭘⭘⭘	Shade in $\frac{5}{6}$ of the circles. ⭘⭘⭘⭘⭘⭘ ⭘⭘⭘⭘⭘⭘
What number does point N represent? 0 ⊢——⊢——⊢——⊢ 1 N	How many hours are there in $\frac{3}{4}$ of a week?	Shade in $\frac{7}{12}$ of the circles. ⭘⭘⭘⭘⭘⭘ ⭘⭘⭘⭘⭘⭘
Write the letter N under the location for $\frac{1}{4}$. 0 ⊢—⊢—⊢—⊢—⊢—⊢—⊢ 1	How many minutes are in $\frac{5}{6}$ of an hour?	How many inches are in $\frac{3}{4}$ of a yard?

Game 29

$\frac{1}{5}$ of an hour = _____ minutes.	40¢ is what fraction of a dollar? (lowest terms)	$\frac{1}{5}$ of a dollar = _____ cents.
$\frac{2}{3}$ of an hour = _____ minutes.	Pencils cost 15¢. Pens cost 60¢. I bought 10 items. The number of pens I bought is $\frac{1}{4}$ the number of pencils I bought. What did I buy?	$\frac{1}{5}$ of a quarter = _____ cents.
$\frac{3}{4}$ of an pound = _____ ounces.	How many hours are in $\frac{3}{8}$ of a day?	$\frac{1}{5}$ of a dime = _____ cents.

Game 30

Write 0.016 as a fraction. Put your answer in lowest terms.	$0.8\overline{)48}$ (Do not use a calculator.)	Change this fraction to a decimal. $\dfrac{4}{5}$
Change this fraction to a decimal. $\dfrac{25}{10,000}$	A shirt costs $28.80. If I buy it on sale, the price will be reduced by $\dfrac{1}{4}$. How much will the shirt cost when it is on sale?	Write 0.60 as a fraction. Put your answer in lowest terms.
$0.8\overline{)0.48}$ (no calculator)	Newspapers sell for 45¢ each. How much should I collect if I sell 88 papers?	$8\overline{)4.8}$ (no calculator)

Game 31

$3\overline{)20.4}$	$3\overline{)1.0}$	$7\overline{)29.4}$
$0.003\overline{)9}$	Divide \$12.36 equally among 6 students. What is each student's share?	$4\overline{)0.076}$
$0.8\overline{)1.616}$	$0.05\overline{)10}$	$0.08\overline{)56.24}$

Game 32

Write as a decimal: $\dfrac{125}{100}$	$5.3 - 2.156 =$	What is $\dfrac{1}{1000}$ less than 7.650?
$0.8\overline{)2.424}$	Which is greater: 0.87 or 0.8699?	Write 0.045 as a fraction.
$\begin{array}{r} 1.08 \\ \times\ 0.6 \\ \hline \end{array}$	1.2345 Which digit is the thousandths place? The hundredths place? The tenths place?	True or false? $0.5 = \dfrac{1}{2}$

Tic-Tac-Toe Math

41

Game 33

What is a ratio?	What is the ratio of the hours in a day to the minutes in an hour?	What is a proportion?
What is the ratio of the number of ounces in a pound to the number of pints in a gallon?	You were paid $3.50 per hour in a job. If you earned $21.00, how many hours did you work?	$\dfrac{5}{8} = \dfrac{N}{30}$ $N = $ _____
8 is to 15 as 4 is to _____ .	$\dfrac{2}{N} = \dfrac{3}{9}$ $N = $ _____	3 is to 5 as _____ is to 25.

Game 34

If I drive 55 miles per hour, how far will I travel in 8 hours?	A baseball team wins 3 out of every 4 games. If it plays 60 games, how many will it win?	If I drive 1100 miles at 55 miles per hour, how many hours will I drive?
A recipe for 8 pancakes requires $1\frac{1}{4}$ cups of flour. How many pancakes will 5 cups of flour make?	Two amoebas are placed into a jar of water. Their number doubles every 24 hours. At the end of 14 days the jar is full. When was the jar half full?	The scale on a map indicates 1 cm equals 200 miles. The distance between two cities is 4.5 cm. How far apart in miles are the cities?
My well provides 22 gallons of water per minute. If I run the water for 6 minutes, how many gallons of water will be used?	Three girls can wax a car in 1 hour 15 minutes. At that rate, how long would it take 2 girls to wax a car?	Strawberry pickers earned $1.25 per crate. How many crates had to be picked in order to earn $45.00?

Game 35

1% means _____ ¢ per dollar or _____ dollar per 100 dollars.	What is 1% of $80?	What is 1% of $800?
5% means _____ ¢ per dollar or _____ dollars per 100 dollars.	A book and a pen cost $1.20. The pen costs 50% of the price of the book. How much does each item cost?	What is 5% of $13?
_____% means 10¢ per dollar or _____ dollars per 100 dollars.	What is 10% of $300?	What is 15% of $50?

Game 36

$\frac{1}{2}$ = _____ %	$\frac{1}{5}$ = _____ %	$\frac{1}{4}$ = _____ %
$\frac{2}{5}$ = _____ %	Circle 75% of this word: GEOMETRY	$\frac{3}{4}$ = _____ %
$\frac{1}{3}$ = _____ %	$\frac{1}{10}$ = _____ %	$\frac{1}{100}$ = _____ %

Game 37

Shade 25% of the square.	What is percent?	Write 8% as a decimal.
Write 45% as a fraction in lowest terms.	Twenty students are enrolled in a class. Fourteen of them are absent. What percent of the students are attending class?	$\frac{7}{20}$ = _____ %
What percent is shaded?	I made 6 out of 20 shots in a basketball game. What percent did I make?	A quiz contains 8 questions. You get 7 correct. What percent do you get correct?

Name_____

Game 38

20% is what fraction? (lowest terms)	$A \to B$ represents what percent of this drawing?	20% is what decimal?
	A B C D E F	
What is 20% of $5?	If September began on a Monday, which day of the week represents 20% of September? What would the date be?	20 is what percent of 50?
25 is 20% of _____ .	If 20% of $1 is 20¢, what is 20% of $15?	A test contains 20 questions. You miss 4. Circle your test score. 75% 50% 80% 90% 60%

Game 39

Nine months is what percent of a year?	Two dimes and 3 pennies is what percent of a quarter?	What percent of a yard is 18 inches?
What percent of a mile is 1320 feet?	I worked 40 hours at $4.65 per hour. I put 30% of the total earnings into a savings account. What amount of money did I place in savings?	What percent of a ton is 500 pounds?
What percent of a day is 18 hours?	Two pints is what percent of a gallon?	What percent of a meter is 60 millimeters?

Measurement Concepts

Game 40

How many ounces are in 1 pound?	How many quarts are in 1 gallon?	How many inches are in 1 yard?
How many pints are in 1 quart?	A box of graham crackers weighs 8 ounces. It takes 3 crackers to weigh 1 ounce. How many crackers are in the box?	How many seconds are in 24 hours?
It is 8:30 AM. What time will it be in $7\frac{1}{2}$ hours?	How many pounds are in 1 ton?	How many eggs are in 1 gross?

Game 41

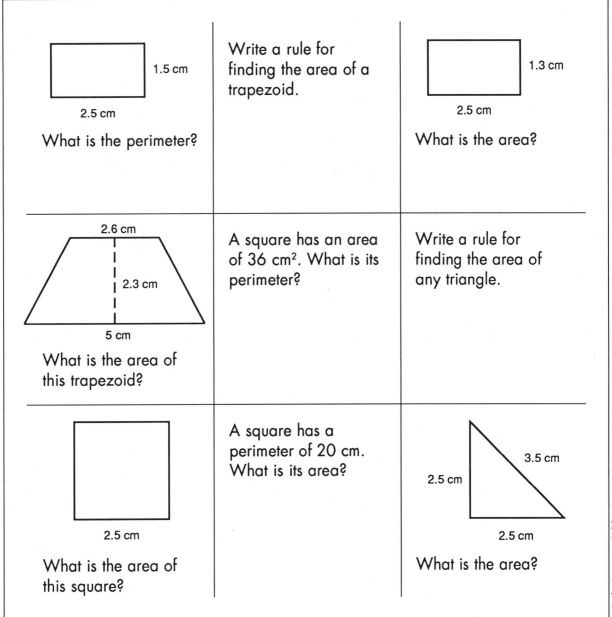

1.5 cm

2.5 cm

What is the perimeter?

Write a rule for finding the area of a trapezoid.

1.3 cm

2.5 cm

What is the area?

2.6 cm

2.3 cm

5 cm

What is the area of this trapezoid?

A square has an area of 36 cm². What is its perimeter?

Write a rule for finding the area of any triangle.

2.5 cm

What is the area of this square?

A square has a perimeter of 20 cm. What is its area?

3.5 cm

2.5 cm

2.5 cm

What is the area?

© Dale Seymour Publications

Game 42

Draw a radius in this circle.

Define *circumference.*

Draw a diameter in the circle.

A rule to use to find

_____

is to multiply 3.14 by the diameter of a circle.

2 cm

radius = _____
diameter = _____
area = _____

1.5 cm

circumference = _____

Write the symbol for pi.

What decimal number is commonly used to represent pi?

To find the area of a circle, what do you multiply?

Tic-Tac-Toe Math

Game 43

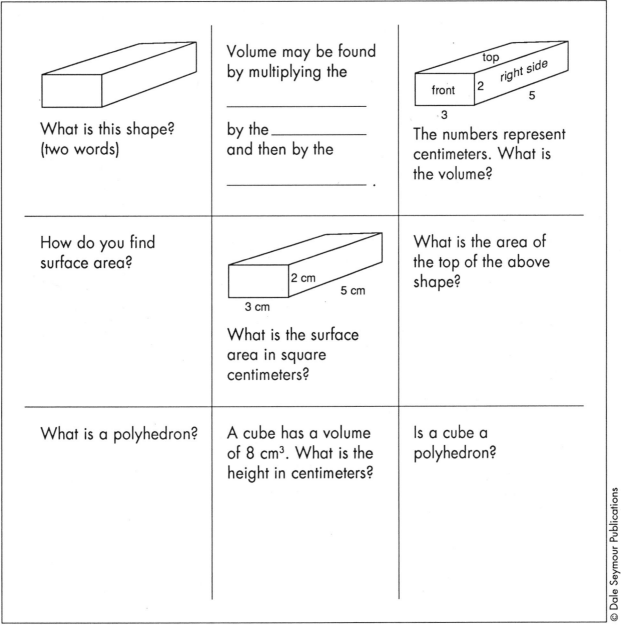

What is this shape? (two words)

Volume may be found by multiplying the

_____

by the _____ and then by the

_____ .

The numbers represent centimeters. What is the volume?

How do you find surface area?

What is the surface area in square centimeters?

What is the area of the top of the above shape?

What is a polyhedron?

A cube has a volume of 8 cm³. What is the height in centimeters?

Is a cube a polyhedron?

Game 44

Measure this line in inches. _____	What is the measure of N? 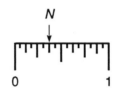 0 1	Measure this line to the nearest centimeter. _____
Measure this triangle. perimeter = _____ cm 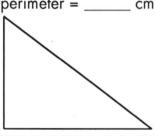	The area of a rectangle is 120 cm². The length is 7 cm longer than the width. What are the dimensions of the rectangle?	The distance from M to N is _____ cm. 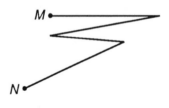
Measure the sides to the nearest centimeter. What is the area of this rectangle? 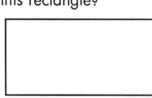	The scale on a map indicates that 1 cm = 250 miles. How many centimeters would represent 1500 miles?	17 mm = _____ cm

Name _____

Game 45

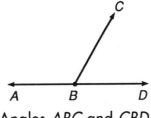

What is the measure
of ∠ABC?

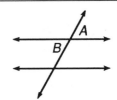

Angles ABC and CBD

are _____
angles.

Angles such as ABC
and CBD will give a

sum of _____ degrees
when measured and
added together.

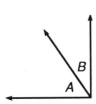

If angle A is 55°,
what is angle B?

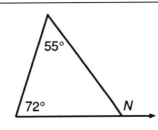

What is the measure
of angle N?

If angle A has a
measure of 60°, how
much is angle B?

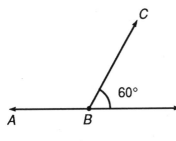

Angles A and B are

called _____
angles because the
sum of their measures
equals 90°.

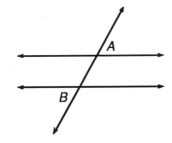

If angle B measures
60°, what is angle A?

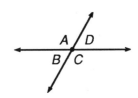

What is the sum of the
measures of the four
angles?

© Dale Seymour Publications

Tic-Tac-Toe Math

Game 46

How many square inches are in 1 square foot?	How many square feet are in 1 square yard?	How many cubic feet are in 1 cubic yard?
How many square feet are in 1 acre?	A gallon of paint covers 500 ft². How many gallons are needed to paint the walls in a room 24 ft long, 16 ft wide, and 7 ft high?	How many cubic yards of cement will be needed to pour a floor 6 in. deep, 24 ft wide, and 36 ft long?
How many tons of hay are in 150 bales if each bale weighs 60 pounds?	Cement costs $49 per cubic yard for the first 10 cubic yards, and $48 per cubic yard after that. What is the price of the cement in the middle right side problem?	A cement truck can haul 9 cubic yards of cement at a time. How many trips will it take to deliver enough cement for the above problem?

Geometry

Game 47

These lines are called
_____ lines.

These lines are
_____ .

The name of this angle
is a_____
angle. It has exactly
_____degrees.

This angle has less
than 90 degrees.
It is called an
_____ angle.

There are _____
degrees in a circle.

This angle has more
than 90 degrees. It is
an_____angle.

How many degrees
does this angle have?

Estimate the number of
degrees in this angle.

This is the symbol for
a line.
What is this symbol
called?

Game 48

What is a polygon?	What is a 3-sided polygon called?	What is a polygon called that has 4 sides, right angles, and all sides congruent?
What does *congruent* mean?	Name four different kinds of triangles.	What is a 5-sided polygon called?
What is a 6-sided polygon called?	What is an 8-sided polygon called?	Is a square a rectangle?

Problem Solving

Game 49

I feed my puppy 3 meals each day. How many meals will the puppy eat in 30 days?	My puppy eats 20% of a can of dog food at each meal. How many meals will 3 cans of dog food provide?	How many cans of dog food should I purchase to feed my puppy for 30 days?
Dog food costs 65¢ per can. How much will it cost to feed my puppy during the month of September?	Which brand of dog food is least expensive? Canine Plus: $0.65 for an 8-oz can Puppy Yup: $1.30 for a 15-oz can Wow Chow: $1.59 for three 6-oz cans	My allowance is $5 each week. How much money will I have left at the end of September if I buy Canine Plus dog food?
I spend $2\frac{1}{2}$ hours each week with my puppy. One-third of this time is used to train her. How many minutes each week do I train her?	I take my puppy on a $\frac{1}{4}$ mile walk each weekday and a $\frac{1}{3}$ mile walk twice a day on weekends. How far do we walk during 1 week?	My puppy weighs 2 lb. She will be fully grown at 20 lbs. If she gains 2 oz each day, how many days will it take my puppy to reach her maximum weight?

Game 50

A piece of wood is 14 ft long. When I cut it into 2 pieces, one of the pieces is 4 ft longer than the other. What are the lengths of the two pieces?	A 12-ft board is cut into 3 pieces—*A*, *B*, *C*. *A* is 1 ft longer than *B*. *B* is $\frac{1}{2}$ ft shorter than *C*. What are the lengths?	A board is 20 ft long. It will be cut into 4 pieces. Each piece will be 2 ft longer than the piece cut just before it. What will be the lengths of the 4 pieces?
A string is cut into 8 equal lengths. Each length is 12 in. How long was the string before it was cut?	A rectangle has a length of 8 ft and a width of 4 ft. If I double the length and the width, by how many times will the area increase?	A rectangle has an area of 32 ft². What is the largest perimeter possible for this rectangle? (The length and width are whole numbers.)
A rope is cut into 5 lengths. The longest piece is 3 ft 6 in. long. Each piece of rope is 8 in. shorter than the next longer piece. How long was the rope before it was cut?	A 15-ft ladder has rungs 15 in. apart. The first rung is 15 in. from the ground. The last rung is 15 in. from the top of the ladder. How many rungs does the ladder have?	How many feet above the ground am I if I am standing on the eighth rung?

Tic-Tac-Toe Math

Game 51

A mother bird brings 4 insects per hour to her young. The father bird catches $1\frac{1}{2}$ times as many. How many insects does this bird family eat in 8 hours?	A pet parakeet eats a treat pellet every 6 hours. There are 20 pellets in a box. How many days before the bird eats all the pellets in the box?	There are 128 oz of liquid in a gallon. If there are 8 oz in 1 cup, how many cups are in 1 gallon?
If a tree grows at a rate of 6 in. per year, how old is a tree that is 72 ft tall?	If $A = 1¢$ $B = 2¢$ $C = 4¢$ $D = 8¢$ and if this pattern continues, how much is the word MATHEMATICS worth?	Instructions on a medicine bottle: Take one tablet per day for 3 days, then two per day for 3 days, then one per day. How many tablets are needed for 10 days?
A doctor told me to drink 9 cups of water per day. My glass holds $\frac{3}{4}$ cup of water. How many of these glasses of water must I drink in a day to get 9 cups of water?	If a slice of bread has 70 calories, how many calories are in a loaf of bread that has 20 slices?	A recipe says to beat the cake batter $2\frac{1}{2}$ minutes at 350 strokes per minute. How many strokes will it take to beat the cake batter?

Statistics

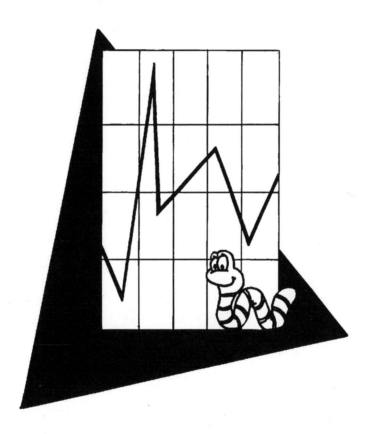

Game 52

What is a mode?	Six students had the following amounts: 35¢, 10¢, 25¢, 20¢, 20¢, 15¢. range = _____ mode = _____ median = _____	What is a median?
A pair of dice were rolled 5 times. These sums occurred: 12, 7, 7, 8, 9. What is the mean for these data?	The mean for a set of data is 150. Find the missing number in the data. 150, 160, 140, 180, _____	Here are some test scores: 75%, 90%, 60%, 80%, 90%, 30%. Which is greater, the median or the mean?
How do you find the mean?	25, 15, 25, 30, 10, 32, 30, 12, 25 mode = _____ median = _____	How do you find the range?

Game 53

I scored these points in 8 basketball games: 20, 20, 16, 21, 15, 20, 14, 10. range = _____ mean = _____ median = _____ mode = _____	I earned these amounts: $2.50, $3.75, $6.20, $3.75, $8.00, $5.75. How much greater is the mean than the mode?	I worked these hours in 1 week: 8, $6\frac{1}{2}$, 5, 8, $5\frac{1}{2}$, 7, $7\frac{1}{2}$, 8. Which is greatest, the mean, mode, or median?
Five baseball players hit these many home runs in a season: 36, 25, 45, 23, 8. What is the median for these data?	What 4 numbers have a range of 4, a median of 22, a mean of 22, and a mode of 22?	Is there a mode in this data: 3, 4, 5, 6, 7, 8?
Students received these test scores: 96%, 88%, 52%, 75%, 82%, 91%, 75%. What is the mean?	These numbers were on a lottery ticket: 18, 33, 42, 17, 26. What is the range?	I have 5 numbers. The mean for these numbers is 12. What is the sum of the numbers?

Probability

Game 54

What is probability?	If I flip an American penny, what is the probability of getting heads?	A bag contains 3 green, 2 red, and 1 yellow cube. What is the probability of drawing out a red cube?
What is the probability of spinning *B*?	If I roll 2 dice 36 times, what is the predicted probability of getting a sum of 7?	If I roll a die, what is the probability of getting a 6?
What is the probability of getting a tails-tails combination if I flip 2 pennies?	There are 52 cards in a deck. What is the probability of drawing an ace?	What is the probability that Christmas day is December 25 (in America)?

Tic-Tac-Toe Math

Game 55

I have 4 dimes, 3 nickels, and 5 pennies in my pocket. I draw out 1 coin at random. What is the probability of drawing out a nickel?	If this were a spinner, what is the probability of getting a 2? 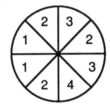	Two pennies are tossed. What is the probability that one coin will be heads and the other tails?
What is an outcome?	A lottery uses 1-digit numbers (such as 4, 6, 5). What is your probability of choosing 3 numbers correctly? (The digits may be repeated.)	I am rolling 2 dice and adding the two numbers. How many outcomes are possible?
What is the probability of rolling a sum of 12 on 2 dice?	What is the probability that the first 2 children born into a family will be boys?	On a true-false test, what is the probability of getting all questions correct by guessing, if there are only 3 questions?

Algebra

Game 56

Name the coordinates. 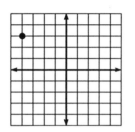	The line that looks like this on the graph  is the horizontal _____.	Name the coordinates. 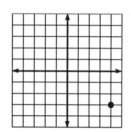
Each graph has four sections. What is each section called?	Place a dot on –3,5. 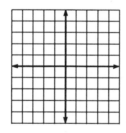	The exact center of the graph is called the _____.
Name the coordinates. 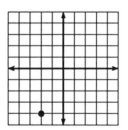	The line that looks like this on the graph 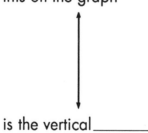 is the vertical_____.	Name the coordinates. 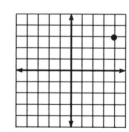

Game 57

5 + (–2) =	–5 + (–2) =	5 – (–2) =
–5 – (–2) =	Describe what happens when you subtract a negative number.	–9 + 12 =
6 – (–1) =	–3 + 4 =	6 + (–1) =

Game 58

What is an integer?	$-8 \cdot (-5) =$	A negative integer multiplied by another negative integer equals a _____ integer. (negative or positive)
$3 \cdot 2 = 6$ $3 \cdot 1 = 3$ $3 \cdot 0 = 0$ $3 \cdot (-1) =$ $3 \cdot (-2) =$ $3 \cdot (-3) =$	Start with -5. Multiply by -8. Subtract -10. Add 20. What is the number?	$-1 \cdot 3 = -3$ $-1 \cdot 2 = -2$ $-1 \cdot 0 = 0$ $-1 \cdot (-1) =$ $-1 \cdot (-2) =$ $-1 \cdot (-3) =$
A positive integer multiplied by a negative integer equals a _____ integer. (negative or positive)	$8 \cdot (-5) =$	The temperature is 5 degrees above zero. The temperature drops 8 degrees. What is the temperature after it drops?

Game 59

A negative integer divided by a negative integer equals a _____ integer. (negative or positive)	$(-5)^2 =$	A negative integer divided by a positive integer equals a _____ integer. (negative or positive)
$-16 \div 4 =$	Start with –2. Multiply by 8. Divide by –4. Subtract 3. What is the number?	$-16 \div (-4) =$
$-4 \cdot 3 \cdot (-2) =$	Which is greater, –8 or 1?	$10 \div (-2) \cdot 3 =$

Game 60

What is a variable?	Write this equation in words. Then solve it. $4N = 30$	Write an equation for this problem: If I multiply 3 by a number, the result is 18.
Write in words. Then solve. $\frac{N}{5} = 6$	A number added to itself and then multiplied by 9 will give a result of 270. What is the number?	$2y - 4 = 12$ $y =$
$3N + 6 = 21$ $N =$	What is an expression?	If I divide a number by 3 and then add 8, the result is 13. Write an equation. Then solve.

Game 61

x	y
3	9
5	25
8	64

Function: y =

x	y
27	3
9	1
18	2

y =

x	y
4	13
5	16
8	25

y =

x	y
10	19
5	9
8	15

y =

x	y
2	8
3	27
4	64

y =

x	y
8	4
10	5
5	$2\frac{1}{2}$

y =

x	y
1	9
5	33
4	27

y =

x	y
1	6
2	9
3	14

y =

x	y
215	8
30	3
121	4

y =

Tic-Tac-Toe Math

79

© Dale Seymour Publications

Game 62

Function: $y = x^2$	Function: $y = x^2 + 1$	Function: $y = x^2 - 2$

x	y
0	
	4
7	

x	y
2	
	37
5	

x	y
9	
12	
	98

Function: $y = \frac{1}{2}x$	Function: $y = x^3$	Function: $y = 2x + 5$

x	y
4	
8	
24	

x	y
2	
3	
4	

x	y
1.5	
4	
3.1	

Function: $y = x \div 3$	Function: $y = x + 2$	Function: $y = x - 1$

x	y
9	
30	
5	

x	y
50	
	32
0.8	

x	y
75	
	49
0	

Miscellaneous Problems

Game 63

How many $\frac{1}{4}$ hours are there in $3\frac{1}{2}$ hours?	$3\frac{1}{2} \times 2\frac{1}{3} =$	Jennifer is 12. Perlita is 13. In 25 years, what will be the product of their ages?
12.3456 Which digit is the tenths digit?	A restaurant has tables for 4 and tables for 6. A total of 32 tables will seat 152 customers. How many tables for 6 are there?	What two prime numbers add together to give a sum that equals 2^3?
$5^3 + 4^2 =$	You work 3 days per week from 8:00 AM to 1:30 PM. You earn $6.50 per hour. How much do you earn in 2 weeks?	$\dfrac{\Box}{\Box} \times \dfrac{2}{3} = 1$

Game 64

0.325 = ____ %	Show how 28 is a triangular number.	Mai-Ling gets a $15 raise. This is 5% of her salary. What was her old salary? What is her new salary?
☐ x 5 + 15 = 360	Eight hundred plants were sold in a fundraiser. Our school received 40% of the sales. If plants sold for $3.00 each, how much money did our school raise?	My bank balance starts out at $50.00. I write checks for $2.59, $18.03, and $11.87. I deposit $23.02. What is my new balance?
List the first four cubic numbers.	$\frac{1}{4} + \frac{1}{3} \times \frac{1}{2} =$	One milkshake and 3 sandwiches cost $9.00. Two shakes and 2 sandwiches cost $10.00. Three shakes and 1 sandwich cost $11.00. What is the cost of 1 sandwich?

Game 65

$\square^3 = 1728$	Add: 3 hrs 45 min 15 sec 2 hrs 30 min 50 sec 1 hr 25 min 20 sec	$\square^2 = 225$
A soccer player takes 20 shots and makes 12. What percent does the player make?	A frog ate 104 insects in 4 days. Each day it ate 10 more than on the previous day. How many insects did the frog eat on each day?	$\sqrt{361}$
ABCDABCD . . . If this pattern continues, what would be the one hundredth letter?	How many centimeters are in 1 meter?	A leaky roof allows 2 drops of water through the first day, 4 drops the second day, 8 drops the third day, and so on. On which day does the five hundredth drop fall through?

Tic-Tac-Toe Math

Game 66

A test contains 20 problems. You get only 5 correct. What percent do you miss?	$\dfrac{3}{4} - \dfrac{\square}{\square} = \dfrac{1}{3}$	A swim team has 27 meets. It wins 5 more meets than it loses. How many meets does it win?
Write 36,000 in scientific notation.	Three boys have $108. Dave has $3 more than Murray. Murray has twice as much as Yoshio. How much does each boy have?	Write 2352 in scientific notation.
Two blocks weigh 56 pounds. One block is 6 times heavier than the other block. How much does each block weigh?	5 ——> 26 3 ——> 10 7 ——> 50 9 ——> ____ 2 ——> ____ ____ ——> 65 Fill the blanks with correct solutions.	$\dfrac{1}{4}\quad\dfrac{2}{12}\quad\dfrac{3}{4}\quad\dfrac{1}{9}$ $\dfrac{6}{7}\quad\dfrac{5}{4}\quad\dfrac{5}{6}\quad\dfrac{2}{3}$ Circle the two fractions above that will give the greatest product.

Game 67

List all factors of today's date (day of the month).	Write a fraction. $0.003 = \dfrac{\square}{\square}$	1, 3, 6, 10 . . . If this pattern continues, what would be the tenth number in the sequence?
$3^2 - 5 =$	Tacos sell for $0.55 each. You buy some and give the clerk $5.00. You get back $0.60 in change. How many tacos did you buy?	What is $\frac{5}{6}$ of 30?
$\begin{aligned} &\frac{1}{2} \\ -\,&\frac{2}{5} \\ \hline \end{aligned}$	What three consecutive numbers add up to 66?	$\frac{1}{2} \div \frac{2}{5} =$

Game 68

Write as a number: eighteen thousand five and two hundredths.	You start a newspaper route that has 21 customers. If you get 3 new customers a week, how many weeks will it take to double your starting number of customers?	Fifty pounds of potatoes cost $6.85. How much do 20 pounds of potatoes cost?
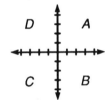 Which letter represents the quadrant in which –3,2 is located?	$A + B = 112$ A is 4 more than C. B is 2 less than C. What does C equal?	Find two square numbers that give a sum of 74.
Give the next three answers: A, 2, D, 5, G, 8,	$\frac{1}{3}$ of my number is 12. $\frac{1}{4}$ of my number is 9. What is $\frac{1}{6}$ of my number?	What is the reciprocal of $\frac{3}{4}$?

Answer Key

Game 1

999	20	388
30	1152	34
70	16,929	60

Game 3

687	4309	153
16	36	Multiply $N \times N \times N$ (N^3)
7	79,049	(9)

Game 2

55	24	38
20	820	2004
152	24,498	5

Game 4

38	23	a number that immediately follows in sequence, e.g., 1, 2, 3 . . .
5	One example: $8 - 6 = 2$ $9 - 5 = 4$ $4 - 2 = 2$ $2 + 1 = 3$	26, 27, 28
12	83	16

Game 5

23	6	10
45	put parentheses around (96 + 6 – 4) or (96 + 6)	6
8	0	172

Game 7

$2.44	$7.00	$7.03
$195.50	2 sandwiches 3 apples 1 milk	$1.78
$78.37	$6.75	about 220 hours

Game 6

9, 6	an answer to an addition problem	3, 13
an answer to a multiplication problem	6, 12	an answer to a subtraction problem
3, 9	an answer to a division problem	2, 6

Game 8

8 hours	369	$140
$2.47	$17.72	83
126	$19.35	$17.50

Game 9

$0.80 for 2 lbs	4 at $0.24 each	$250 at 20% off
$110 at 10% off	8 hours	77¢
38¢	c. $24.50 for 10 hours	$2.80

Game 11

the amount of money borrowed	the amount of money charged when you borrow money	a percent charged for borrowing the money
$p \times r \times t$ principal x rate x time	$61.53 or $61.54	$198
$144	$32.50	$2464

Game 10

the total amount earned before deductions are made	the amount received after deductions are taken out	$142.50
$169.10	$213.75	$45.10
$150.90	26	20%

Game 12

Monday	0 hours 30 minutes	6:30 AM
86,400	12:30 PM	1440
52	366	September, April, June, November

Game 13

6 hours 20 minutes	14 years 3 months	12:00 noon
5:00 PM	$5.20	3:10 PM
210 minutes	$7\frac{1}{2}$	9:30 PM

Game 15

Answers will vary. Use this game as a discussion activity to help students think about the cost of consumer items.		

Game 14

$1.68	5.9	8
2.055	$38.00 for 10 hours	20
$125	$0.80	1700

Game 16

the product of an integer and itself	204	a small number written above and to the right of another number that tells how many times to multiply itself
2	5	3
9	125	10

Game 17

2	27	64
10	$163.84	8
3	100	4

Game 19

123,400	(6 x 1000) + (2 x 100) + (5 x 10) + (6 x 1)	5×10^3
1, 2, 3, 4, 6, 8, 12, 24	23, 29, 31, 37	d. 2 x 3 = 6
c. 10	a. 6	c. 4

Game 18

1, 2, 3, 4, 6, 8, 9, 12, 18, 24, 36, 72	8, 16, 24, 32, 40, 48	1, 2, 4, 5, 8, 10, 20, 40
6, 12, 18, 24, 30, 36	36	24
8	2, 3, 5, 7, 11, 13, 17, 19	a number with exactly 2 factors: itself and 1

Game 20

c. 16	$2^2 \times 5^2$	c. 6
c. 12	1, 2, 4	c. 12
c. 1000	no	4.225×10^3

Game 21

24	11, 19, 41	1, 4, 9, 16, 25, 36
$2^2 \times 3^2$	10, 25	1, 3, 6, 10
36	45 or 54	2×5^2

Game 23

numerator	$\frac{3}{4}$	the bottom number of a fraction
$\frac{3}{4}$	$\frac{6}{8}, \frac{12}{16}, \frac{9}{12}, \frac{75}{100}$	$\frac{5}{3}$
0.75	$1\frac{2}{3}$	denominator

Game 22

13, 16, 19	48, 96, 192	15, 21, 28
$\frac{1}{16}, \frac{1}{32}, \frac{1}{64}$	25, 36, 49	1.2, 1.5, 1.8
C, X, D	□ △ ○	−1, −3, −5

Game 24

1	$\frac{7}{12}$	2
$\frac{7}{12}$	24	$\frac{1}{4}$
3	$\frac{3}{4}$	4

Game 25

$\dfrac{5}{12}$	$\dfrac{3}{4}$	$\dfrac{1}{4}$
$\dfrac{15}{8}$	$\dfrac{9}{16}$	$5\dfrac{2}{5}$
$3\dfrac{1}{12}$	40	$8\dfrac{1}{3}$

Game 27

$\dfrac{3}{10}$, 0.3	$\dfrac{15}{100}$, 0.15	0.006
3.0003	0.55 or equivalent decimals	$\dfrac{1}{2}$
$\dfrac{8}{1000}$	5.0008	$7\dfrac{1}{20}$

Game 26

$1\dfrac{1}{4}$ or 1.25	$\dfrac{1}{2}$	$\dfrac{3}{8}$ or 0.375
0.75	45	$1\dfrac{1}{2}$ or 1.5
$0.75	9	16

Game 28

8 circles shaded	9 circles shaded	10 circles shaded
$\dfrac{3}{4}$	126 hours	7 circles shaded
	50	27

Game 29

12	$\dfrac{2}{5}$	20
40	8 pencils, 2 pens	5
12	9	2

Game 31

6.8	$0.3\overline{3}$	4.2
3000	$2.06 each	0.019
2.02	200	703

Game 30

$\dfrac{2}{125}$	60	0.8
0.0025	$21.60	$\dfrac{3}{5}$
0.6	$39.60	0.6

Game 32

1.25	3.144	7.649
3.03	0.87	$\dfrac{45}{1000}$ or $\dfrac{9}{200}$
0.648	4, 3, 2	true

Game 33

a comparison of two quantities	$\frac{24}{60}$ or $\frac{2}{5}$	two ratios that are equivalent
$\frac{16}{8}$ or $\frac{2}{1}$	6	$18\frac{3}{4}$ or 18.75
$7\frac{1}{2}$ or 7.5	6	15

Game 35

1, 1	$0.80	$8.00
5, 5	pen = $0.40, book = $0.80	$0.65
10, 10	$30.00	$7.50

Game 34

440 miles	45	20
32	at the end of the thirteenth day	900 miles
132	50 minutes	36

Game 36

50	20	25
40	(GEOMET) RY	75
$33\frac{1}{3}$	10	1

Game 37

 teacher observation	part of a hundred	0.08
$\frac{9}{20}$	30%	35
50%	30%	$87\frac{1}{2}$ %

Game 39

75%	92%	50%
25%	$55.80	25%
75%	25%	6%

Game 38

$\frac{1}{5}$	20%	0.2 or 0.20
$1.00	Saturday, September 6	40%
125	$3.00	80%

Game 40

16	4	36
2	24	86,400
4:00 PM	2000	144

Game 41

8 cm	A = (base + base) x height ÷ 2	3.25 cm²
8.74 cm²	24 cm	A = base x height ÷ 2
6.25 cm²	25 cm²	3.125 cm²

Game 43

rectangular prism	length, width, height	30 cm³
Find the area of each side. Add the areas.	62 cm²	15 cm²
3-dimensional solid object with 4 or more surfaces	2 cm	yes

Game 42

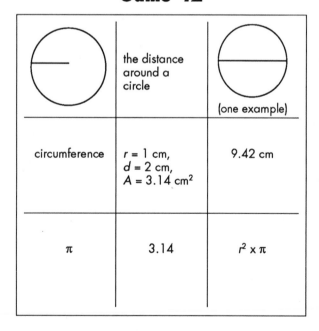

	the distance around a circle	(one example)
circumference	r = 1 cm, d = 2 cm, A = 3.14 cm²	9.42 cm
π	3.14	r^2 x π

Game 44

$1\frac{5}{8}$ inches	$\frac{3}{8}$ inches	3
12	15 cm by 8 cm	11 cm
8 cm²	6	1.7

Game 45

120°	supplementary	180°
35°	127°	60°
complementary	60°	360°

Game 47

parallel	perpendicular (also intersecting)	right, 90
acute	360	obtuse
90	45 (estimate)	ray

Game 46

144	9	27
43,560	Between 1 and 2 gallons	16
4.5	$778	2

Game 48

a closed-plane figure made of straight lines	triangle	square
same size, same shape	right, scalene, equilateral, isosceles	pentagon
hexagon	octagon	yes

Game 49

90	15	18
$11.70	Canine Plus	$8.30
50	$2\frac{7}{12}$ miles	144

Game 51

80	5	16
144 years	$13,193.18	13
12	1400	875

Game 50

9 ft and 5 ft	4.5 ft, 3.5 ft, 4 ft	2 ft, 4 ft, 6 ft, 8 ft
96 in.	4	66 ft (length = 32, width = 1)
130 in. or 10 ft 10 in.	11 rungs	10 ft

Game 52

The number in a set of data that occurs most often	range = 25, mode = 20, median = 20	middle of a set of data
8.6	120	median (77.5)
Add all numbers in the set of data. Divide by the amount of numbers.	mode = 25, median = 25	Subtract smallest number in the data from the largest.

Game 53

range = 11, mean = 17, median = 18, mode = 20	$1.24	mode
25	20, 22, 22, 24	no
about 80% (79.85)	25	60

Game 55

$\frac{3}{12}$ or $\frac{1}{4}$	$\frac{3}{8}$	$\frac{2}{4}$ or $\frac{1}{2}$
the way something can happen	$\frac{1}{1000}$	36
$\frac{1}{36}$	$\frac{1}{4}$	$\frac{1}{8}$

Game 54

chance	$\frac{1}{2}$	$\frac{2}{6}$ or $\frac{1}{3}$
$\frac{3}{4}$	$\frac{6}{36}$ or $\frac{1}{6}$	$\frac{1}{6}$
$\frac{1}{4}$	$\frac{4}{52}$ or $\frac{1}{13}$	1

Game 56

−4,3	axis	4,−3
quadrant	teacher observation (left 3, up 5)	origin
−2,−4	axis	4,3

Game 57

3	–7	7
–3	You add the inverse.	3
7	1	5

Game 59

positive	25	negative
–4	1	4
24	1	–15

Game 58

any whole number and its opposite	40	positive
–3, –6, –9	70	1, 2, 3
negative	–40	–3

Game 60

a letter or other symbol that represents a number	4 multiplied by a number equals 30. $N = 7.5$	$3N = 18$
A number divided by 5 equals 6. $N = 30$	$2n \cdot 9 = 270$ $18n = 270$ $n = 15$	$y = 8$
$N = 5$	a number sentence such as $n + 3$ or $4y$	$\dfrac{N}{3} + 8 = 13$ $N = 15$

Game 61

$y = x^2$	$y = \dfrac{x}{9}$	$y = 3x + 1$
$y = 2x - 1$	$y = x^3$	$y = \dfrac{x}{2}$
$y = 6x + 3$	$y = x^2 + 5$	$y =$ Add digits of x

Game 63

14	$8\frac{1}{6}$	1406
3	12	3 and 5
141	$214.50	$\dfrac{3}{2}$

Game 62

Function: $y = x^2$	Function: $y = x^2 + 1$	Function: $y = x^2 - 2$

x	y
0	0
2	4
7	49

x	y
2	5
6	37
5	26

x	y
9	79
12	142
10	98

Function: $y = \frac{1}{2}x$	Function: $y = x^3$	Function: $y = 2x + 5$

x	y
4	2
8	4
24	12

x	y
2	8
3	27
4	64

x	y
1.5	8
4	13
3.1	11.2

Function: $y = x \div 3$	Function: $y = x + 2$	Function: $y = x - 1$

x	y
9	3
30	10
5	$\frac{5}{3}$

x	y
50	52
30	32
0.8	2.8

x	y
75	74
50	49
0	−1

Game 64

32.5%	$1 + 2 + 3 + 4 + 5 + 6 + 7$	$300, $315
69	$960	$40.53
1, 8, 27, 64	$\dfrac{5}{12}$	$2.00

Game 65

12	7 hrs 41 min 25 sec	15
60%	11, 21, 31, 41	19
D	100	ninth day

Game 67

Answers depend on the date.	$\frac{3}{1000}$	55
4	8	25
$\frac{1}{10}$	21, 22, 23	$1\frac{1}{4}$

Game 66

75%	$\frac{5}{12}$	16
3.6×10^4	Yoshio = $21, Murray = $42, Dave = $45	2.352×10^3
48 and 8 pounds	82, 5, 8; Rule = $N^2 + 1$	$\frac{6}{7}$, $\frac{5}{4}$

Game 68

18,005.02	7	$2.74
D	55	49 and 25
J, 11, M	6	$\frac{4}{3}$